The Job Hunting Handbook
by Harry Dahlstrom

The Job Hunting Handbook

ISBN 978-0-940712-27-0

Printed in the United States of America

Published by

Dahlstrom & Company, Inc.
50 October Hill Road
Holliston, MA 01746
Tel: 1-800-222-0009
www.DahlstromCo.com

Cover photography

Shutterstock
Copyright, Arthimedes

Design

ChrisHerronDesign.com

Special thanks

Deb Holmes, Ann Keenan, Jamie Dahlstrom, Gail Dahlstrom, Chris Herron, Susan Plawsky, Andy Peterson, Lindsay Dahlstrom, and the office pooch Scout

Free job-hunting tools and the latest national hiring trends at www.HarryDahlstrom.com

Contents

Welcome to the American job market

The American job market is one of the most exciting marketplaces in the world. It's a place where millions of people compete for work. It's a place where careers are launched, where fortunes can be made, and where dreams can come true.

Is there a job out there for you?

Of course there is. As you can see from the chart below, employers hired 70 million people in 2020. That's the same as they hired the year before in 2019.

But what the chart doesn't show is that there are millions of people on permanent or temporary layoff due to the coronavirus.

As the virus restrictions ease and people start looking for new jobs or better jobs, competition for those jobs will increase. There could be dozens, even hundreds, of people competing for every job you want.

Don't let the competition frighten you

Most job hunters are not very organized and they don't have a plan. Too many people think job hunting means sitting in front of a computer, filling out a dozen job applications, crossing their fingers for luck, and waiting for an employer to call them. For most, no one ever calls.

You may not know this, but employers who are financially healthy are always looking for good people to hire. Even during the worst recessions, it's amazing how quickly a hiring freeze will thaw when the right person starts chipping away at the ice.

Annual hires, in millions of people

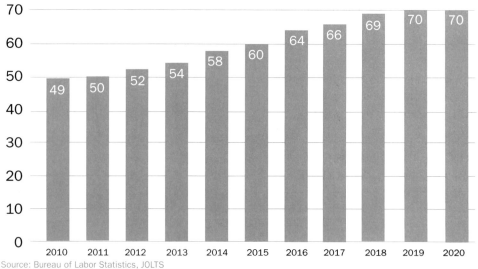

Source: Bureau of Labor Statistics, JOLTS

How can you become that person employers want to hire?

Here's the plan—

· Learn how employers hire so you'll know what they really need and want

· See how to turn the employer's job requirements into your list of accomplishments in three easy steps—even if you're a first-time job hunter

· Just fill in the blanks to create a resume that shows you are qualified and hirable

· Discover the top-three ways to get job interviews— plus four more— just in case

· How to set up a long, steady, stream of job interviews that can keep you busy for weeks and weeks to come

· Make a great impression by showing a little personality and answering 50 tough interview questions with ease

· Know how to dress, act, show enthusiasm, why they matter— and so much more

This is easier than you think

You can do this. Everything you need is right here in this little book. Each chapter is short and to the point. The language is simple and friendly, with a dash of humor. You can also read this book in an hour or so and get started today.

Now, take a peek at page 6 and you'll see that there are job openings for your occupation

Then turn to page 8 and you'll see how employers hire, so you can find out what they really want— and become the solution they're looking for.

FIRST THINGS FIRST

Before we get started, if you're new to the job market or if you're thinking about switching to a different line of work, you need to choose a specific occupation.

If you apply for a job without naming a specific occupation, some employers will put you where they need you. This means you'll run the risk of getting stuck in a job you'll hate, stuck in a dead-end job with no chance for advancement, or stuck in a job with frequent layoffs and no job security. Don't let some stranger decide your future. Take charge of your life and choose your own occupation.

Here are six easy ways to choose an occupation:

· Start with your wish list. What kind of work have you always dreamed of doing?

· Think about your friends and relatives. Do you know people who have the kind of jobs you'd like to have?

· Think about the things you love to do. Do you have a hobby or a passion that you could turn into an occupation?

· Think about your talents. Do you have a special talent, skill, or ability that could be turned into an occupation?

· Try a career test. Log onto a computer and Google "career tests." Career tests analyze your personality by asking a few dozen multiple-choice questions. Then, they match your personality to occupations you'd be good at. Give it a try. You might be surprised at what they recommend. Most tests are free, so try several different tests. Caution—use the test results only as a guide, not a rule. No test is totally accurate.

· Need some help choosing an occupation? Contact a career counselor at your school or your local American Job Center. Career counselors will not choose a career for you. But, they could administer some special aptitude tests and help you explore some options. To find a job center near you, Google, American Job Centers or One Stop Career Centers

Wages & Demand For The 175 Largest U.S. Occupations Through 2028

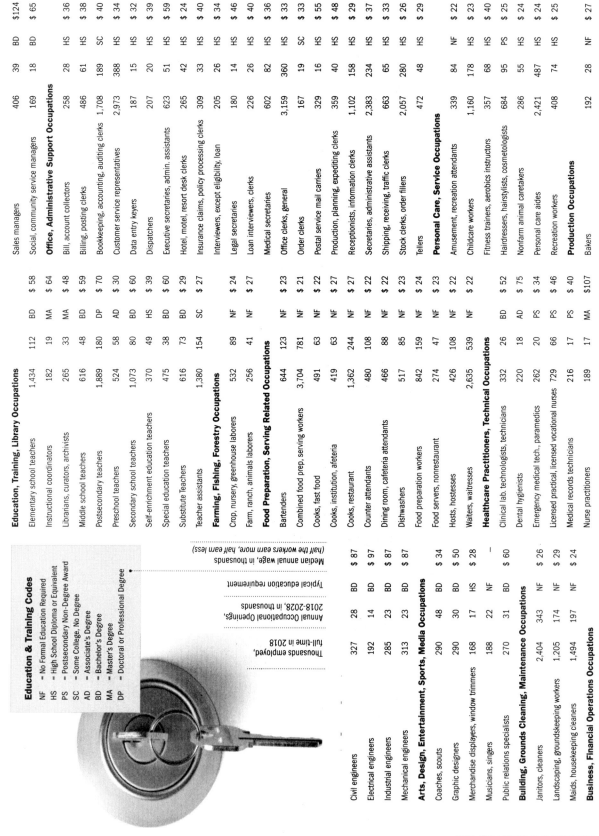

Column key:
- Thousands employed, full-time in 2018
- Annual Occupational Openings, 2018-2028, in thousands
- Typical education requirement
- Median annual wage, in thousands (half the workers earn more, half earn less)

Occupation	Thousands employed, full-time in 2018	Annual Occupational Openings 2018-2028 (thousands)	Typical education requirement	Median annual wage (thousands)
Civil engineers	327	28	BD	$87
Electrical engineers	192	14	BD	$97
Industrial engineers	285	23	BD	$87
Mechanical engineers	313	23	BD	$87
Arts, Design, Entertainment, Sports, Media Occupations				
Coaches, scouts	290	48	BD	$34
Graphic designers	290	30	BD	$50
Merchandise displayers, window trimmers	168	17	HS	$28
Musicians, singers	188	22	NF	–
Public relations specialists	270	31	BD	$60
Building, Grounds Cleaning, Maintenance Occupations				
Janitors, cleaners	2,404	343	NF	$26
Landscaping, groundskeeping workers	1,205	174	NF	$29
Maids, housekeeping cleaners	1,494	197	NF	$24
Business, Financial Operations Occupations				
Education, Training, Library Occupations				
Elementary school teachers	1,434	112	BD	$58
Instructional coordinators	182	19	MA	$64
Librarians, curators, archivists	265	33	MA	$48
Middle school teachers	616	48	BD	$59
Postsecondary teachers	1,889	180	DP	$70
Preschool teachers	524	58	AD	$30
Secondary school teachers	1,073	80	BD	$60
Self-enrichment education teachers	370	49	HS	$39
Special education teachers	475	38	BD	$60
Substitute Teachers	616	73	BD	$29
Teacher assistants	1,380	154	SC	$27
Farming, Fishing, Forestry Occupations				
Crop, nursery, greenhouse laborers	532	89	NF	$24
Farm, ranch, animals laborers	256	41	NF	$27
Food Preparation, Serving Related Occupations				
Bartenders	644	123	NF	$23
Combined food prep, serving workers	3,704	781	NF	$21
Cooks, fast food	491	63	NF	$22
Cooks, institution, afeteria	419	63	NF	$27
Cooks, restaurant	1,362	244	NF	$27
Counter attendants	480	108	NF	$22
Dining room, cafeteria attendants	466	88	NF	$22
Dishwashers	517	85	NF	$23
Food preparation workers	842	159	NF	$24
Food servers, nonrestaurant	274	47	NF	$23
Hosts, hostesses	426	108	NF	$22
Waiters, waitresses	2,635	539	NF	$22
Healthcare Practitioners, Technical Occupations				
Clinical lab. technologists, technicians	332	26	BD	$52
Dental hygienists	220	18	AD	$75
Emergency medical tech., paramedics	262	20	PS	$34
Licensed practical, licensed vocational nurses	729	66	PS	$46
Medical records technicians	216	17	PS	$40
Nurse practitioners	189	17	MA	$107
Sales managers	406	39	BD	$124
Social, community service managers	169	18	BD	$65
Office, Administrative Support Occupations				
Bill, account collectors	258	28	HS	$36
Billing, posting clerks	486	61	HS	$38
Bookkeeping, accounting, auditing clerks	1,708	189	SC	$40
Customer service representatives	2,973	388	HS	$34
Data entry keyers	187	15	HS	$32
Dispatchers	207	20	HS	$39
Executive secretaries, admin. assistants	623	51	HS	$59
Hotel, motel, resort desk clerks	265	42	HS	$24
Insurance claims, policy processing clerks	309	33	HS	$40
Interviewers, except eligibility, loan	205	26	HS	$34
Legal secretaries	180	14	HS	$46
Loan interviewers, clerks	226	26	HS	$40
Medical secretaries	602	82	HS	$36
Office clerks, general	3,159	360	HS	$33
Order clerks	167	19	SC	$33
Postal service mail carriers	329	16	HS	$55
Production, planning, expediting clerks	359	40	HS	$48
Receptionists, information clerks	1,102	158	HS	$29
Secretaries, administrative assistants	2,383	234	HS	$37
Shipping, receiving, traffic clerks	663	65	HS	$33
Stock clerks, order fillers	2,057	280	HS	$26
Tellers	472	48	HS	$29
Personal Care, Service Occupations				
Amusement, recreation attendants	339	84	NF	$22
Childcare workers	1,160	178	HS	$23
Fitness trainers, aerobics instructors	357	68		$40
Hairdressers, hairstylists, cosmetologists	684	95	PS	$25
Nonfarm animal caretakers	286	55	HS	$24
Personal care aides	2,421	487	HS	$24
Recreation workers	408	74	HS	$25
Production Occupations				
Bakers	192	28	NF	$27

Occupation	Employment (000s)	Openings (000s)	Education	Median Wage ($/hr)
Accountants, auditors	1,424	146	BD	$ 71
Buyers, purchasing agents	432	40	BD	$ 63
Claims adjusters, examiners, investigators	329	26	HS	$ 66
Compliance officers	320	31	BD	$ 69
Cost estimators	217	24	BD	$ 64
Financial analysts	330	31	BD	$ 86
Human resources specialists	626	68	BD	$ 61
Loan officers	316	30	BD	$ 63
Logisticians	175	18	BD	$ 75
Management analysts	876	100	BD	$ 84
Market research analysts, specialists	682	91	BD	$ 63
Personal financial advisors	272	23	BD	$ 89
Training, development specialists	306	37	BD	$ 61
Community, Social Service Occupations				
Child, family, school social workers	340	37	BD	$ 46
Clergy	234	28	BD	$ 49
Educational, vocational counselors	325	37	MA	$ 56
Healthcare social workers	181	22	MA	$ 56
Social, human service assistants	414	58	HS	$ 34
Substance abuse counselors	305	42	BD	$ 45
Computer, Mathematical Occupations				
Computer network support specialists	191	17	AD	$ 63
Computer programmers	250	15	BD	$ 84
Computer systems analysts	634	53	BD	$ 89
Computer user support specialists	672	65	SC	$ 51
Network, computer systems administrators	384	29	BD	$ 82
Software developers, applications	944	99	BD	$104
Software developers, systems software	421	35	BD	$110
Web developers	161	15	AD	$ 69
Construction, Extraction Occupations				
Carpenters	1,007	116	HS	$ 47
Cement masons, concrete finishers	191	23	NF	$ 43
Construction laborers	1,405	179	NF	$ 36
Electricians	715	95	HS	$ 55
Operating engineers	402	53	HS	$ 48
Painters, construction, maintenance	376	41	NF	$ 39
Plumbers, pipefitters, steamfitters	500	66	HS	$ 54
Pharmacists	314	14	DP	$126
Pharmacy technicians	420	38	HS	$ 33
Physical therapists	248	17	DP	$ 88
Physicians, surgeons	757	29	DP	$208
Radiologic technologists	211	14	AD	$ 60
Registered nurses	3,060	210	BD	$ 72
Healthcare Support Occupations				
Dental assistants	346	45	PS	$ 39
Home health aides	832	141	HS	$ 24
Medical assistants	687	100	PS	$ 34
Nursing assistants	1,513	191	PS	$ 29
Installation, Maintenance, Repair Occupations				
Automotive service technicians, mechanics	770	74	PS	$ 41
Bus, truck mechanics	285	28	HS	$ 47
HVAC mechanics, installers	368	43	PS	$ 48
Industrial machinery mechanics	382	38	HS	$ 52
Maintenance, repair workers, general	1,488	157	HS	$ 38
Telecom equipment installers, repairers	233	24	PS	$ 56
Legal Occupations				
Lawyers	824	46	DP	$121
Paralegals, legal assistants	326	40	AD	$ 51
Management Occupations				
Administrative services managers	300	28	BD	$ 96
Architectural, engineering managers	193	15	BD	$141
Chief executives	263	17	BD	$190
Computer, information systems managers	414	39	BD	$143
Construction managers	472	40	BD	$ 93
Education administrators, K-12	275	23	MA	$ 95
Education administrators, postsecondary	193	17	MA	$ 94
Farmers, ranchers, agricultural managers	975	96	HS	$ 68
Financial managers	654	65	BD	$128
Food service managers	356	47	HS	$ 54
General, operations managers	2,376	230	BD	$101
Industrial production managers	187	14	BD	$103
Marketing managers	259	26	BD	$134
Medical, health services managers	406	42	BD	$100
Property, real estate, association managers	363	32	HS	$ 58
Cutting, punching, press machine operators	189	19	HS	$ 34
Electrical, electronic, assemblers	280	31	HS	$ 34
Helpers--production workers	355	58	HS	$ 28
Inspectors, testers, sorters, samplers, weighers	574	54	HS	$ 38
Laundry, dry-cleaning workers	219	29	NF	$ 23
Machinists	395	42	HS	$ 44
Packaging, filling machine operators	395	47	HS	$ 30
Printing press operators	176	16	HS	$ 36
Welders, cutters, solderers, brazers	425	49	HS	$ 41
Protective Service Occupations				
Correctional officers, jailers	434	34	HS	$ 44
Firefighters	332	25	PS	$ 50
Police, sheriff's patrol officers	687	53	HS	$ 61
Security guards	1,144	154	HS	$ 28
Sales, Related Occupations				
Cashiers	3,649	661	NF	$ 22
Counter, rental clerks	436	59	NF	$ 27
Insurance sales agents	476	53	HS	$ 51
Parts salespersons	258	31	NF	$ 30
Real estate sales agents	369	39	HS	$ 49
Retail salespersons	4,511	641	NF	$ 24
Sales reps, wholesale, manufacturing	1,406	151	HS	$ 59
Sales reps, technical, scientific products	326	36	BD	$ 80
Securities, financial services sales agents	442	45	BD	$ 64
Telemarketers	168	21	NF	$ 25
Transportation, Material Moving Occupations				
Bus drivers, school or special client	498	66	HS	$ 32
Bus drivers, transit, intercity	184	25	HS	$ 42
Cleaners of vehicles, equipment	409	64	NF	$ 25
Driver/sales workers	448	49	HS	$ 25
Heavy, tractor-trailer truck drivers	1,959	238	PS	$ 44
Industrial truck, tractor operators	615	73	NF	$ 35
Laborers, material movers, hand	2,954	435	NF	$ 28
Light truck or delivery services drivers	1,001	121	HS	$ 33
Packers, packagers, hand	673	93	NF	$ 25
Taxi drivers, chauffeurs	370	51	NF	$ 26

Source, U.S. Bureau of Labor Statistics

Learn how employers hire so you'll know what they need and want

Hiring new employees is tricky. First, it's expensive. It costs employers about $4,000 to recruit and train each new person. Second, finding someone with the right skills and personality can be difficult. One out of five new hires is a disappointment. Here's the process that hiring managers use to find the best candi-

1. The hiring manager begins the process by reviewing and updating the job description

A job description is a document that explains the duties needed to perform a job. Every job has a job description.

The hiring manager will rely on that job description when writing help-wanted advertisements, reading resumes, screening job hunters, and conducting job interviews.

You might say that the job description is a yardstick. Anyone who applies for the job is measured against it.

2. The job opening is announced

Most hiring managers will announce the job opening to their employees first. They know that some employees might want to apply for that job opening themselves.

Other employees might know some outside friends who would be a great fit for that job opening. These friends of employees are a hiring manager's favorite source for above-average applicants.

It's often said that 60 to 80 percent of all job openings are never advertised to the public. That's because current employees and friends of employees get the jobs before the openings ever go public.

55% of the labor force work for small businesses
26% of the labor force work for medium-size businesses
19% of the labor force work for large businesses

Small = under 100 employees, Medium = 100-499 employees, Large = 500 employees or more

—U.S. Census Bureau

Still, if a hiring manager wants to see additional job hunters, she can always post the job opening on the employment page of her company's website. She can also post help-wanted advertisements with job boards, attend job fairs, host open-house events, and request resumes from career centers and employment agencies.

3. Job applications and resumes come pouring in

When job hunters apply for a job online, their applications and resumes are read by a computer. The computer is programmed to ignore applications and resumes that do not meet the job's specific requirements.

Sadly, more than half of all applications and resumes do not have the "right stuff" and the computers reject them.

In smaller companies that don't have applicant-tracking software, the manager will give each application and resume a quick ten-second glance. The manager is primarily looking for the five or six important requirements listed in the job description. Managers can tell in a glance if the application or resume has the right stuff or not.

4. Phone calls are made

When the hiring manager receives an application or resume with the right stuff, she'll phone the job hunter. This phone call is a screening call.

During the call, the manager will ask questions about the job hunter's experience and availability. If she thinks this person might be a good fit for the job, the job hunter will be invited to visit the company for a face-to-face job interview.

5. Interviews are scheduled

Hiring managers want to personally meet the five or six people who pass their telephone interviews. They want to drill down into each job hunter's skills and accomplishments. They want to see how solid they are. They also want to get a fix on their personalities. Hiring managers try not to hire difficult people.

Of the five or six people interviewed for the job, two finalists usually stand out.

6. References are checked

The hiring manager will contact each of the two finalists' references. She will also contact their former schools and employers to verify their education and employment claims.

Some managers will even visit their blogs, Facebook, Linkedin, and Twitter sites to get a sense of their personalities and interests.

After evaluating the two finalists, one person usually stands out.

7. The job is offered

Finally, the hiring manager gets to make the phone call we all want to hear, "I would like to invite you to join our team."

Once the yahoos and screams of joy have subsided, wages, benefits, and a starting date are discussed. Medical examinations and deeper background checks are also scheduled.

And that's how the hiring manager gets her guy or gal.

HOW LONG DOES IT TAKE FOR AN EMPLOYER TO HIRE SOMEONE?

In a study of over 300,000 job interviews, the job site, Glassdoor, reports that the average time needed to evaluate a job candidate is 22.9 days.

But, those 22.9 days can fluctuate by industry, employer size, and occupation. Here are seven industries and the typical days needed to screen a job applicant:

Average time to evaluate a job candidate

Industry	Days
· Government	60
· Hospital	32
· College/university	30
· Nonprofit	28
· Public corporation	23
· Franchise	11
· Private corporation	9

Small employers do respond faster than large employers. Small employers respond in about 15 days. Medium-size employers average about 20 days. Large employers can average 26 days.

The complexity of the job can also affect hiring times. Police officers, for example, have the longest hiring time at 127.6 days. Food servers and bartenders have one of the shortest hiring times at 5.7 days.

Show the employer that you have the "right stuff"

Every occupation has certain requirements. Carpenters must know how to read building plans. Sales people must know how to close a sale. Customer-service people must know how to work with difficult people. Managers must know how to motivate people to get the job done. What's the right stuff for your occupation? Don't guess. Find out. Show that you have the specific skills employers are looking for. Here's how—

Let's take it from the beginning

I'm sure you know what a portrait photographer does. So, let's use that occupation in the following example—

1. Name the job you want

· Portrait photographer

2. List the requirements of the job from the help-wanted ad

· Capture the personality of the person

· Set up the equipment for the photo shoot

· Create the setting to get the best shot

· Position and coach the subject

· Schedule appointments to view photo proofs and sell photo packages

3. Select the first requirement from your list

· Capture the personality of the person

4. Give an example of when or where you performed it

· While at Wolcott Studio, I learned a valuable technique for capturing natural facial expressions

5. Add some details

· I ask questions, capture 35-45 candid facial expressions on each client and increase sales by 10%

6. Repeat steps 3, 4, and 5 for each additional job requirement on your list

· ·

"Lack of technical skills," is the number-one reason employers have trouble filling job openings

—Manpower

Where can you find the job requirements for your occupation?

If you are responding to an advertisement or a job posting, look for a statement in the ad that says, "The ideal candidate will be able to ..." or "Job duties include ...." That's where the hiring managers tell you exactly which job requirements they want. Those requirements come straight from their job descriptions.

If you are not responding to a specific advertisement and you want a general idea of your occupation's requirements, visit several job sites, like Indeed, Careerbuilder, Linkedin, and Monster. Then, read a dozen help-wanted advertisements for your occupation. Pick out the 5 common job requirements that all the ads seem to want. That's the stuff most hiring managers are looking for.

You can also dig out those job requirements in the US Department of Labor's, *Occupational Outlook Handbook*. It includes the job descriptions for hundreds of different occupations. It's free online at http://www.bls.gov/ooh/.

How much detail should you include?

Mention the important facts but keep them short and simple. Also try to include numbers to describe the volume, percent, size, money, time, effort, or the result of what you did. Facts and numbers are specific. They allow the managers to visualize what you accomplished.

Instead of saying, "I capture beautiful facial expressions," say— "I ask questions, capture 35-45 candid facial expressions on each client and increase sales by 10%

Oh—don't get into the why or how of each project. That's the back-story. Save those interesting details for your job interview.

Now, you try it.

1. **Name the job you want**

   _____

2. **List the job requirements**

   1st _____

   2nd _____

   3rd _____

   4th _____

   5th _____

3. **Select the** 1st **job requirement from your list above**

   _____

   _____

4. **Give an example of when or where you performed it**

   _____

   _____

   _____

5. **Add details**

   _____

   _____

   _____

   _____

   _____

   _____

Continued on the next page—

HERE ARE A FEW EXAMPLES FROM DIFFERENT OCCUPATIONS THAT YOU CAN USE TO HELP TURN YOUR PAST PROJECTS INTO THE "RIGHT STUFF"

SHORT-ORDER COOK

Select a requirement
Make sandwiches

Give an example
Made custom sandwiches in a mobile deli

Add details
Created 15-20 handmade sandwiches, an hour, in a 2-person mobile deli— Ruebens, Cubans, Muffalettas...

OFFICE RECEPTIONIST

Select a requirement
Schedule appointments

Give an example
Scheduled appointments in a busy dental office

Add details
Scheduled appointments in a 3 dentist office serving 200 patients monthly

IT TECHNICIAN

Select a requirement
Improve website quality and usability

Give an example
Re-wrote shopping-cart code to simplify customer experience

Add details
Re-wrote shopping-cart code that reduced customer abandoned orders by 8%

· ·

Select a 2nd requirement from your list on page 11

_____

_____

Give an example of when or how you performed it

_____

_____

_____

Add details

_____

_____

_____

_____

_____

Select a 3rd requirement from your list

_____

_____

Give an example of when or how you performed it

_____

_____

_____

Add details

_____

_____

_____

_____

_____

TECH SUPPORT SUPERVISOR

Select a requirement
Supervise personnel

Give an example
Supervised tech support team at a retail store

Add details
Supervised tech-support team of 7 people who resolved about 900 retail cases a month

EMERGENCY MED TRAINER

Select a requirement
Train and coach

Give an example
Trained and coached a military squad

Add details
Trained and coached a military squad to provide life-saving emergency-medical treatment in combat: gunshot wounds, explosives, bone fractures, burns, more

ASSISTANT BOOKKEEPER

Select a requirement
Assist with accounts payable and accounts receivable

Give an example
Assisted bookkeeper with AP and AR for a retail store

Add details
Assisted bookkeeper with AP and AR for a retail store with over 500 accounts and annual sales of $2 million.

Select a 4th requirement from your list

_____

_____

Give an example of when or how you performed it

_____

_____

_____

Add details

_____

_____

_____

_____

_____

Select the 5th requirement from your list

_____

_____

Give an example of when or how you performed it

_____

_____

_____

Add details

_____

_____

_____

_____

_____

Congratulations!

You just turned the job requirements into your accomplishments. Accomplishments impress employers. They show that you are the kind of person who delivers results.

Use the "right stuff" to build a powerful resume

Looking for a job? Then, you need a resume. Your resume is your calling card, your advertisement, your brochure, your flyer. It's a one-page handout that shows what a great catch you are.

What can you do with a resume?

Mail it. Email it. Post it online. Ask friends to give it to their managers. Hand it out at job fairs. Give it to employment agencies.

The idea is to get your resume into the hands of as many hiring managers as you can. If a hiring manager likes what she sees in your resume, you'll get invited to a job interview.

What if you're not a good writer?

That's okay. Writing your resume is easy. You completed all the heavy thinking in the last chapter. All that's left to do is type it up.

Is there an official format or design you must follow?

No. There is no official format for writing your resume. You can set up your resume any way you like. Feel free to change, modify, expand, ignore, or simplify any of the following suggestions. But, most people do include the following topics in their resumes—

1. Your contact information

Tell employers who you are and how they can reach you—

At the top of the page, type your name, address, cell/text or phone/email, and maybe a link to your blog, Linkedin, or Facebook site. See page 29 before adding your media site.

2. Your goal

In one short sentence, tell what kind of work you want—

- "Seeking full-time position as a dragon slayer."

- If you have little or no experience, say that

Eighty-seven percent of hiring managers say it's important to tailor your resume to the needs of the job.

—Society for Human Resource Management

you are, "Seeking a full-time, entry-level position as a dragon slayer."

3. Your education

Start with your most recent school or program.

- On the first line in this section, give the award, certification, or the degree you earned plus the date of the award. If you haven't graduated yet, simply give the number of credits earned toward your degree (36 credits earned toward a BS degree in magic).

- On the second line, give the school's name and city/state address.

- On the third line, list any classes or activities you participated in that might interest an employer.

- Repeat for additional schools.

4a. Work experience

Start with your most recent employer.

- On the first line in this section, give your job title plus your beginning and ending dates of employment. If you are still employed there, give your starting date and the word "Present" to show that you still hold that job.

- On the next line, give the employer's name and city/state address.

- On the next few lines, list the five or six job requirements with examples from your past (see your notes on pages 11-13).

- Repeat for additional employers.

4b. No work experience?

Instead of a "Work Experience" section, create a section titled, "Accomplishments."

- On the first line in this section, name one of the job requirements.

- Under that job requirement, offer some substitute examples from school, sports, volunteering, or other life projects to show what you achieved in that area (see Substitute Skills on page 11 and the sample resume with no work experience on page 16).

5. Your skills list

Create a section called "Skills."

Then, simply list the names of any important tools, devices, programs, procedures, skills, licenses, and systems that you can operate or perform.

6. Additional information

Create a section called "Additional Information."

You don't have to include this section in your resume. It's optional. But, it is a great place to mention any special talents, abilities, or awards that might interest an employer.

· ·

On the next few pages, you'll find three resumes that you can use to model your resume on.

Notice how simple and clean they look. Bold headings, short sentences, and plenty of white space help the requirements jump off the page. Plus, each job requirement is phrased as an accomplishment with an example of what the person did and numbers to show the size of the projects.

Creating your easy-to-scan resume is even simpler than you think. Just use the fill-in-the-blank worksheet on page 19.

Here's a sample resume showing no work experience

James B. Jobless
1 Hereicome Highway, Ourtown, US 00000
Cell/Text: 111/222-3333   james@myblog.com

GOAL

Seeking an entry-level position in retail sales at a hardware store

EDUCATION

High School Diploma, 06/2020

Hometown High School, Ourtown, US 00000
- Enjoyed classes in math, shop, and computers

ACCOMPLISHMENTS

Although I have no prior experience in retail sales, I believe the following accomplishments show that I could learn the job quickly—

Math Skills
- Maintained 3-year "B" average in algebra and geometry
- Managed $1,000 investment that earned 4.2% APR

People Skills
- Played checkers most Sunday afternoons with seniors at a nursing home
- Formed study group with 4 people to boost grades in French

Product Knowledge
- Automotive: My father is a mechanic and we rebuilt my '99 Volvo including the engine, brakes, and suspension
- Electronics: Programmed family's TV, BlueRay, music, and WI-FI to run on one remote
- Construction: Helped my aunt rebuild a 100 sq/ft screened-in porch on her home

Selling
- Sold my '99 Volvo and earned a $120 profit
- Sold magazines door-to-door for charity, raised $300

ADDITIONAL INFORMATION
- Reliable—Missed only two days of school this year
- Honest—Returned $20 check-cashing error to my bank

Here's a sample resume showing only classroom experience

Lindsay U. Needajob
2 Icandoit Drive, Ourtown, US 00000
Cell/Text: 111/222-3333 Lindsay@mylinkedin.com

GOAL
Seeking a full-time position in public relations with a non-profit organization

EDUCATION
BS in Communications, 06/2020
Beatrice Hart College, Ourtown, US 00000
- Enjoyed classes in Sociology, Journalism, Economics

ACCOMPLISHMENTS

Writing Skills
- Wrote 2,000 word feature story on, "How to Buy a Good Used Car"
- Wrote 500 word short piece on, "Why Lottery Winners Go Bankrupt After Winning Millions Of Dollars"

Public Speaking
- Presented a 10-point technical talk on how to "Recover Data after Your Hard Drive Crashes"
- Appeared in a 30-minute, on-campus TV talk-show, "How to Live on the Money You Have"

Research
- Polled 86 licensed drivers on, "Why People Throw Trash out of Their Car Windows While Driving."
- Analyzed survey data on, "Will There be a Good Job for Me After Graduation?"

Press Relations
- Persuaded local newspaper editor to join a symposium on, "Who's Writing the Rules of Grammar for Texting?"

SKILLS
Microsoft Word, Excel, PowerPoint, Acrobat, WordPress

Note: All work projects cited in this resume were college-course assignments. Writing samples are available on request.

USE ACTION WORDS

Certain words evoke confidence and authority. When offering examples of your past job requirements, be sure to start each sentence with an action word, like:

Achieved…
Assembled…
Assisted…
Built…
Cleaned…
Completed…
Convinced…
Created…
Delivered…
Designed…
Developed…
Equipped…
Established…
Experienced…
Guided…
Handled…
Learned…
Led…
Maintained…
Managed…
Operated…
Organized…
Performed…
Planned…
Produced…
Programmed…
Reduced…
Repaired…
Served…
Set up…
Sold…
Supervised…
Taught…
Trained…
Wrote…

Here's a sample resume showing work experience

Chris O. Hiremenow
3 Gimmeachance Road, Ourtown, US 00000
111/222-3333   chris@myfacebook.com

GOAL

Seeking a position as a finish carpenter

EDUCATION

Vocational Certificate in Fine Carpentry, 06/2016

Tiger Maple Institute, Ourtown, US 00000

- Classes in architectural styles, technical drawing, furniture and cabinet making

Diploma, 06/2014

Shastany Vocational Technical High School, Ourtown, US 00000

- Classes in construction techniques, hand tools, shop equipment

WORK EXPERIENCE

Finish Carpenter, 06/2016 to Present

Hugh's High-End Homes, Ourtown, US 00000

- Duplicated existing English-style, oak-paneled walls for 350 sq/ft library expansion
- Designed and built 6'x9' replica Greek Revival fireplace mantle with hand-carved appliques
- Restored lower half of an Art-Deco staircase damaged by floodwaters
- Remodeled 20'x15' kitchen in the Nantucket style with deep coffered ceilings, bead-board cabinets, and wide pine floors
- Restored 12' high, salvaged antique Victorian doorway to original specifications

Assistant Finish Carpenter, 06/2014 to 06/2016

Arlene's Average Abodes, Ourtown, US 00000

- Installed windows, doors, trim, kitchen box cabinets, stairways, mantles on 15 homes

Intern, 01/2014 to 06/2014

Build'em Up Houses, Ourtown, US 00000

- Helped install windows, doors, trim, and hardwood floors on 3 new homes

SKILLS

Replication, restoration, replacement, modification, design-build, CAD, hand tools, power tools, shop tools including laser cutters, shapers, planers

ADDITIONAL

Detail oriented, organized, neat, good sense of humor

You Try It

Your full name

Your address, city, state, zip code

Your phone, cell/text, email

GOAL

Name the job you are seeking

_____

EDUCATION

Give your diploma, certificate or degree and the date of award

_____

Give the school's name and city/state address

_____

· List several courses you took

_____

Repeat for additional schools or training

WORK HISTORY

Give your job title with beginning and ending dates

_____

Give your employer's name and city/state address

_____

· Give a job requirement, with an example

_____

· Give another job requirement, with an example

_____

· Give another job requirement, with an example

_____

· Give another job requirement, with an example

_____

· Give another job requirement, with an example

_____

Repeat for additional employers

SKILLS

Name the important tools, devices, procedures, programs, systems, and licenses you can operate or perform

_____

ADDITIONAL

Mention any special talents, abilities, or awards

_____

BASIC RESUME WRITING TIPS

· Use standard 8.5" by 11" white paper

· Keep a one-inch margin on all four sides of the page

· Avoid fancy fonts like outline, script, or other difficult-to-read styles

· Keep sentences short and to the point

• **Bold** or CAPITALIZE important headlines so they stand out

· Single space within sections

· Double space between sections

· Use bullets (·) at the beginning of a list

· Whenever possible, use numbers to show the size, volume, time, money, effort, or result of the projects you worked on

· Proofread for spelling and factual errors

Seven ways to get job interviews

The job interview is your chance to sit down, face-to-face, with a hiring manager and convince her that she should hire you instead of someone else. How do you get a job interview? Here are some tips.

• Employee referrals

Ask anyone you know, "How'd you get your job?" Most will tell you, "A friend helped me get a job where she works."

When an employee recommends, or refers, a friend for a job, that's known as an employee referral.

Hiring managers like to hire the friends of their trusted workers. Nine out of ten hiring managers say it's their best source for recruiting above-average people. Friends are so valuable, some employers will pay a finder's fee to an employee who brings in a new hire.

As the friend of an employee, you'll have some special advantages over an outsider. Your inside employee knows when a coworker is about to leave the job. She knows when the team is short-handed and needs help. She knows when the manager is planning to hire someone new.

Your inside employee can also tell you about the hiring manager—her interviewing style, the issues she is most concerned about, the type of person she wants for the job, the questions she is likely to ask, and the things you can do or say to impress the manager.

And here's a bonus—unlike answering a help-wanted ad or a job posting, where hundreds of people might compete for the job, it's not uncommon for friends to be hired with little or no competition at all.

How to get started:

Make a list of all the people you know who work in the same field or occupation as you. Create that list from your phone contacts, social media, family, friends, relatives, neighbors, and even your old

Three sources account for 76% of all new job hires
- Employee referrals create 39.9%
- Employer career sites create 21.2%
- Job boards create 14.6%

—Jobvite Index

friends. Add to your list as days go by and you remember more names.

Here's a script you can use to call your insiders—

1. Choose the first friend from your list and make the call. Spend a few minutes catching up on the news to rekindle your friendship.

2. Then, mention that you would like to apply for a job where she works.

3. Explain that her company's online job application asks, "Do you have a friend or relative who works at our company?" Ask your friend if it's okay to list her as a friend on your job application.

4. Then, ask a few questions about the hiring manager—her name, personality, interviewing style, the kind of person she tends to hire, questions she is likely to ask, and any important issues you should know about.

5. Finally, ask your friend for a big favor. Ask if she would give your resume and cover letter to her manager and put in a good word for you—just in case something opens up.

Thank your friend for being so helpful. Be sure to let her know when the manager contacts you and invites you to an interview.

Then, move on to the next friend on your list and make the call. Call them all.

• Employer career sites

Do you have a list of employers where you would love to work? Visit their web sites and see what kind of job openings they have.

How to get started:

Start with the first employer on your list. Visit their website and navigate to their employment page or career page.

Look through their job postings. When you find a job that interests you, bookmark that web page so you can find your way back to it later.

Now, reach out to your friends. Ask if they know a mutual friend, a common friend, a friend who works inside that company. Dig—you are more likely to get a job interview if you know an insider.

When you find that inside friend, ask if you could list him as a friend on your job application.

Then, ask a favor. Ask if he would give your resume and cover letter to his manager and put in a good word for you.

Thank your friend for his help. Be sure to let him know when you are contacted by the hiring manager and invited to an interview.

Then, move on to the next employer on your list and repeat the process.

• Job boards

Job boards like CareerBuilder, Monster, Craigslist, Indeed and SimplyHired are very popular ways to find job openings.

But don't stop there. Check your area's online newspapers for help-wanted ads, plus the help ads posted on Facebook, and LinkedIn too.

How to get started:

Apply for the jobs you are qualified to do. Don't waste time applying for jobs you cannot perform. The employer's computers are programmed to ignore weak applications.

Submit a strong job application. Identify the requirements the advertisement says are important and include them in your application. Turn the requirements into your accomplishments by adding details and numbers, see page 10.

Always submit a clean job application. Don't let misspellings, wrong numbers, missing information, and information typed in the wrong spaces disqualify you (see page 32 for help).

To boost your chances of getting a job interview,

CREATE A STEADY STREAM OF JOB INTERVIEWS WITH THE 5/25/100 METHOD

Every employer is not hiring today. You have to knock on a lot of doors to find the ones that are.

Here's a simple plan that takes only an hour or so a day. Give it a try and see how many interviews you can get.

· Monday through Friday, contact five employers every day. That's 25 employers a week, 100 a month. To reach them, use a good mix of all the ideas in this chapter.

· Now, you may not get a job interview the first week or so because it takes time for employers to respond.

· But, after two weeks, your phone should start to ring.

· When you begin to get job interviews, don't stop contacting five new employers every day. Stick with your plan right up until the day you accept a job offer.

· If you do stop, your flow of interviews will dry up in about two weeks. Then it will take you two more weeks to get the pipeline flowing again.

attach your resume and cover letter to your job application. Your resume and cover letter will offer detailed accomplishments plus a touch of personality that a job application cannot include.

• Walk-ins

One of the easiest ways to get a job interview is to look for Now Hiring signs on business buildings, doorways, and billboards.

How to get started:

Walk into the shop, store, or office. Smile, and ask one of the employees if you can fill out a job application. You might say, "Hi, I saw your hiring sign. May I have a job application, please?"

You should also ask, "Which jobs are available? What are the duties of a yodeler? Which days and hours are available?"

As you know, the best way to get a job is to get someone who works inside the company to put in a good word for you. So, ask the employee who gives you the job application if someone from your neighborhood, school, or former employer works there.

If you know the insider, call him when you get home. Mention that you applied for a job where he works. Ask if he would be kind enough to give your resume and cover letter to his hiring manager and put in a good word for you.

If you don't know an insider, contact your friends and relatives. See if they know an insider who might be able to help you.

• Job fairs and open houses

Where can you meet dozens of recruiters, face to face, all in one day, all in one place? Simple. Go to a job fair or a company open house. Recruiters are waiting there to meet you.

Keep in mind that recruiters do not usually hire or interview people at a job fair. The job fair is an opportunity for them to meet job hunters and collect resumes.

Recruiters prefer not to interview at the job fair because the fairs are noisy, fast paced, and there are too many people to interview. So, they usually schedule interviews that take place a few days after the job fair.

To find an event in your area, Google—*Job Fair, Career Fair,* and *Company Open House.* Also, check for open-house announcements in the help-wanted section of your Sunday newspapers. Oh, and check with your school's career center and your state's job center to see if they are planning a job fair (see page 23).

How to get started:

Once you are inside the job fair, walk up to an employer's table or booth.

1. Make eye contact with the recruiter, smile, and say hello. Offer your handshake and introduce yourself.

2. Deliver your "sales pitch" from page 23.

3. Answer the recruiter's questions.

4. Offer the recruiter a copy of your resume.

5. Ask for the recruiter's business card.

6. Ask how you can schedule a job interview.

7. Thank the recruiter for speaking with you, smile, and offer your handshake, goodbye.

When you get home, reintroduce yourself by sending the recruiter a thank-you note and another copy of your resume. The recruiter's contact information is on her business card. Adapt the cover letter on page 24 to fit your needs. A thank-you note shows the recruiter that you are interested in an interview and you took the time to write and ask for one.

• Temporary employment agencies

Temporary employment agencies are match

makers. They bring together employers that need help and job hunters who need work.

Working for a temp agency is a great way to get your foot in the door at a good company. You'll learn new skills, gain experience, make contacts, and build references. Every year, about 9 million people find work through employment agencies—and 79 percent are placed in full-time positions.

How to get started:

Google—*employment agencies* for a list of agencies in your area. You might also ask your friends if they've ever worked with an employment agency. Maybe a friend can recommend a good agency for you.

Call the agency and ask to register for employment. The agent will ask a few questions about your background and skills. If you are a good fit for the agency, the agent will ask you to come in for a meeting.

During the meeting, the agent will go over your resume and ask questions about your skills and abilities. For some occupations, like clerical or graphic design, the agent may ask you to take a skills test to measure your abilities.

The agent will also ask about your needs. Do you want to work for a large company or a small one? How far are you willing to commute? Are you looking for full-time, part-time, or seasonal work? What wage or salary do you expect?

The agent will then try to match you to a job opening with one of their employer clients.

• Job Centers and Career Centers

The six activities we just discussed are do-it-yourself activities. You can use those activities to contact an employer yourself.

But, what if you need some help with your resume, getting interviews, or if you have a difficult matter you need to discuss?

Well, there are employment counselors you can talk to. Here are two great resources that have helped millions of people—

1. American Job Centers. Your state government operates several Job Centers. They are open to the public and their services are free. Google—*American Job Centers* or *One Stop Career Centers* to find a center near you.

2. School Career Centers. Most schools and colleges have career centers. Their services are available to their students and alumni, and their services are also free.

How to get started:

Lots of employers are loyal to local Job Centers and Career Centers. They regularly post job openings and recruit new hires there. Job counselors have good working relationships with recruiters, hiring managers, and business owners.

Visit your Center's online help-wanted site. Search for jobs in your occupation. Build a list of employers with jobs you are qualified to perform and apply for those positions online.

Then, ask to speak with a counselor. See if the counselor can offer you a few referrals. Referrals are the names and addresses of recruiters, hiring managers, and business owners who hire people at the companies you've chosen.

When you have someone's name, send an email, text message, or mail a letter with a copy of your resume to introduce yourself and request an interview. Be sure to mention that you were referred by the job center in the opening paragraph of your letter.

By the way, if you are sending an email, use the body of your cover letter as the text in your email. Include your resume as an attachment. On page 24 you'll see how to write a solid cover letter.

CREATE A 15 SECOND SALES PITCH

A sales pitch is a short speech. It's a 15 second "sound bite" that sells you to hiring managers and anyone who can help you get a job interview.

A good sales pitch includes your name, your occupation, your accomplishments, your goal, and your USP (Unique Selling Point). Your USP is what separates you from the competition.

Spend some time thinking about your sales pitch. Here's an example to go by—

"Hi, my name is Mason Stone."

"I've been an apprentice stone mason for the past year and I've learned both wet and dry masonry."

"I've built walkways, terraces, retaining walls, and patios for residential customers. They've been very happy with my work."

"Now, I'm looking for a full-time junior-masonry job."

"Let me also add that—I'm a hard worker and I give more than a minimum effort. I'm reliable and I'll show up on time every day. I'm a quick learner and I'm easy to coach. I also have a good sense of humor and I get along with people. I would love to interview with your company."

Let AIDA help you write a better cover letter

A cover letter is a personal letter that you send with your resume or job application. It's the first thing the hiring manager sees when she opens your envelope or email. It's your hello, your smile, your chance to create a rapport, your reason for writing.

Not everyone sends a cover letter with their resume or job application

And that's why you should send one. It shows that you're different. It shows that you want the job, you are serious, and you took the time to write.

Send your letter to the proper person

Send your letter to the hiring manager. The hiring manager is usually the manager of the department where you want to work. If you want a job in sales, send your letter to the sales manager. If you want to work in maintenance, send you letter to the maintenance manager. At a small business, send your letter to the owner of the business.

How can you get the hiring manager's name?

If you are getting a referral from a friend, ask your friend for the hiring manager's name and address. Send your letter to that manager by name and title—Ms. Iva Joboffer, IT Manager. Make sure the manager's name, title, and address are accurate and spelled correctly.

If you'd like to write to a company but you don't know the manager's name, call the company. The receptionist who answers your call will be glad to give you the information you need.

If you are responding to an advertisement or job posting that gives no contact person's name, address your letter to "Hiring Manager." Be sure to include a box number or job code if one is given in the advertisement.

Eighty-six percent of executives said cover letters are important when evaluating job candidates.

—National Association of Workforce Development Professionals

How long should your cover letter be?

Keep your cover letter short and simple. One page is perfect.

What should you put into your cover letter?

Four things, also known as AIDA.

The folks who write professional sales letters use a magic formula. It's called AIDA. That's short for—Attention, Interest, Desire, Action.

AIDA sells billions of dollars in goods and services every year. If it can work for business, it can work for you.

So, let's use AIDA to persuade a hiring manager to give you a job interview.

1. Attention

In the very first paragraph of your letter, grab the hiring manager's attention simply by telling her why you are writing.

Below are several solid reasons for writing to a hiring manager. Adapt the ONE that works best for you.

1. "I would like to apply for the sous chef's position I saw advertised in..."

2. "My friend, Frieda Friendly, works in your department. She recommended that I write to you."

3. "I stumbled upon your website. Wow. I'd like to interview for a position with your firm..."

4. "I shop at your store and..."

5. "We met at a job fair on..."

6. "I would like to learn about the career opportunities for mechanics at your shop."

2. Interest

In the second paragraph of your letter, rouse the manager's interest by explaining what makes you special. Here are a few examples. Adapt the ONE that works best for you.

1. "I have three-year's experience as a..."

2. "I worked on the Slingshot project at David's and..."

3. "I just graduated from school and..."

4. "I have three special abilities I can bring to the job..."

5. "I have an idea I'd like to discuss with you..."

3. Desire

If you are responding to a help-wanted advertisement or a job posting, be sure to talk about the job requirements the ad says are important. Otherwise, create a desire for the hiring manager to meet you by offering three solid accomplishments.

1. "I am very familiar with..."

2. "I know how to use..."

3. "I also have experience with..."

4. Action

Finally, ask the hiring manager for a job interview. Adapt ONE of the following statements that works best for you.

1. "I would love to interview for your nursing position. Please call. You can reach me anytime on my cell at 555-666-7777."

2. "I would like to interview for your nursing position. I hope you won't mind if I call in a few days to see that you received my resume and hopefully to schedule an interview."

A sample letter using AIDA

Your name and contact information ▶

Pat Perfect
One Pluperfect Way
Anytown, US 12345
(111) 222-3333
pat@email.com

Date ▶

December 31, 20xx

Hiring manager's name and address ▶

Ms. Karin K. Boom, Owner
New Day Demolitions, Inc.
55 Nowhiring Highway
Anytown, US 12345

Job Code ▶

Re: Job Code 5678, from the *Blabbermouth*

Salutation ▶

Dear Ms. Boom:

Attention ▶

I would like to apply for your Office Receptionist's position, which I saw advertised in Wednesday's edition of the *Blabbermouth.*

Interest ▶

Ms. Boom, I can offer you three years of experience as a receptionist. I have a cheerful helpful personality, and I have a good memory for names, faces, voices, and telephone numbers.

Desire ▶

- I am familiar with most telephone systems, social media, email, plus both Apple and Microsoft operating systems.
- I have hands-on experience with QuickBooks, Microsoft Word, Excel, and appointment scheduling software.
- I also have experience as a bill collector. If the need arises, I would be happy to make collection calls or field difficult or awkward inquiries.

Action ▶

I would love to interview for this position. I hope you'll call. You can reach me anytime on my cell at (111) 222-3333.

When you do call, please understand that the child's voice on my voice-mail greeting is not my voice!

I look forward to your call.

Closing ▶

Sincerely,

Signature ▶

Pat Perfect

Printed name ▶

Pat Perfect

You Try It

Your name
Your address
Your city, state, zip
Your phone number
Your email address

Today's date

Manager's name and title
Department's name
Company's name
Address
City, state, zip

Re: (Job code, if listed in an ad or job posting)

Dear (Mr. or Ms.):

Get the manager's attention

_____

_____

Rouse the manager's interest

_____

_____

Create a desire to meet you

• _____

• _____

• _____

Ask the manager to take action

_____

_____

Sincerely,

Your Signature

Your typed signature

Get ready for the hiring manager's phone call

You've found a job opening and applied for the position. Now, if the hiring manager likes what she sees in your resume, she'll give you a call. Don't underestimate the importance of this phone call. It's actually a screening interview. The purpose of the call is to decide whether to invite you to a face-to-face job interview or not. Here are six tips to help you pass the screening and win an invitation to the interview.

1. Have a professional greeting

You never know when an employer might call, so answer every phone call with a professional greeting. Sure, your friends will laugh when they call and hear you say, "Hello. This is Ken Dooit. How can I help you?" But the hiring managers will love it.

Also, record a new phone message. Something short and professional like this—"Hello. This is Ken Dooit. I'm not able to answer the phone just now. Please leave your name, number, and a brief message. I do check my messages often. I'll return your call as soon as possible. Thank you."

2. When they call you, most hiring managers will ask if this is a convenient time to speak with you

Managers know that you have a life. If you're at work, driving your car, or sitting in the dentist's chair, it's okay to arrange another time to talk.

When you return a manager's call, choose a place where you'll be free from noise, interruptions, and where your cell phone has good reception.

You might say—"Good afternoon, Ms. Hireyou. My name is Ken Dooit. I'm returning your phone call. I applied for a job as a tight-rope walker."

3. Prepare and rehearse like this is a real interview.

Because it is. If you bomb this screening interview, you won't get the face-to-face interview or the job offer.

> Your telephone conversation with a hiring manager could last between ten minutes and an hour.
>
> —*Wall Street Journal*

So, be prepared. Have your resume, cover letter, a copy of the job advertisement, and notes from the employer's website in front of you.

You can't know which questions a hiring manager might ask, so look over these common questions plus those on page 44.

- Are you currently employed? Where?
- What is your job title?
- How long have you been working there?
- What are your duties and responsibilities?
- Tell me about your job skills.
- Do you get along with your supervisor?
- Why are you leaving your job?
- When are you available to begin work?
- Why do you want to work for my company?
- What motivates you to do a good job?
- What are your career goals?

4. Try to relax

The manager knows that her phone call to you will be a surprise. She also knows you'll be nervous. So, she'll conduct the conversation as if it's a casual friendly chat.

Smile—even on the phone. Smiling helps project a personality that comes across in your voice.

You might also standup, pace, or walk around the room while speaking on the phone. Thinking on your feet and gesturing with your hands can help improve your thinking.

5. Use your best manners

Always refer to the manager as Mr. or Ms., unless the hiring manager asks you to use their first name.

Be sure to say please and thank you.

Don't sip a drink, chew gum, or nibble on food. The manager will hear it and it's rude.

Don't use foul or inappropriate language—this is the workplace not the schoolyard.

Try not to say, "No problem," "Uh-huh," "Like," or "Ya know," too often. They can become annoying.

Also, don't ask about wages, benefits, or vacations—they are usually discussed when a job offer is made.

Be willing to accept the hiring manager's interview schedule, even if you have to reschedule the cable guy.

Confirm the date and time of the interview by repeating it back to the hiring manager—"That's Thursday the 13th at 3:13..."

Thank the hiring manager for showing an interest in you—"Ms. Hireyou, thank you so much for this opportunity. I look forward to meeting you on Thursday. Bye."

And here's a big one. Don't take another phone call or try to read incoming text messages during this phone interview. It's rude and some managers will wonder which phone call is more important, theirs or your friend's. So, turn off the dings and rings before your phone interview begins. Let the manager feel that she is your most important caller.

6. What if the manager doesn't offer you a job interview?

Ask for one. That's what this phone call is all about. You might say something as simple as this—"I'm very interested in this position. I would love to visit your company. Could we schedule an interview?"

Find three people who will give you a positive recommendation

You are a good worker. You give more than the minimum. You show up every day and you're never late. You're easy going and everybody likes you. Well, that's great. But the hiring manager wants proof. She wants to talk to three references—three people who can vouch for you.

Who should you include as references?

Most hiring managers want three reliable references. Ideally, they want the name of your current boss—but NOT if that boss doesn't know that you're looking for another job. In that case, they'll want the name of your previous employer.

Other good references might include former supervisors, coworkers, customers, teachers, coaches, and prominent people who know you. Prominent people might include an attorney, a banker, a doctor, a member of the clergy, or a local business owner who knows you.

Always ask before offering someone's name as a job reference

People who agree to serve as references almost always give a better recommendation than those who are not asked.

Those who are NOT asked are often caught off guard. They might struggle to remember who you are, what you did, and when you worked for them. To a hiring manager this hesitation might sound like your reference is not eager to recommend you.

How to ask someone to be a reference—

Call or visit them. Don't ask by text or email. You need to see each person's face or hear their voice when you ask.

Ninety-two percent of organizations do conduct background checks.

—The Society for Human Resource Management

When you do ask, don't just ask for a recommendation. Ask for a positive recommendation.

You might say, "Greta, I'm applying for work as a ballerina. I would like to list you as a reference. Would you be able to give me a positive recommendation?"

Most people are flattered when asked. They'll be happy to give you a good recommendation and they'll say so.

A few might not be interested in singing your praises. So, listen to their voice. Notice their body language. What does your gut tell you? If you don't think they'll give you a good recommendation, don't use them.

What if your former boss won't give you a good recommendation?

Do you have to list him or her as a reference? Could you ask your boss's boss for a recommendation instead? How about your shift supervisor, or a senior coworker?

Or maybe you should just tell the hiring manager that you and your former boss didn't get along.

The hiring manager will admire your honesty.

Here's a big tip—never badmouth a former boss. It screams that you are a troublemaker.

Instead, put a positive spin on a negative situation. Try this: "Mr. Pumpernickel was the most demanding boss I ever worked for. We had our moments. But, I learned more from him than anyone I've ever worked for. I'm going to miss him."

Should you list your references on your resume?

No. If you include your references on your resume, you are inviting hiring managers to call your references before they've even met or interviewed you.

Instead, list your references on a separate sheet of paper.

At the top of the page, give your name, address and phone number so the manager will know who's references they are.

Then, type the words PERSONAL REFERENCES. Beneath that headline, include each person's name, address, phone number, employer, job title, how you know them, and best times for the hiring manager to call each of them.

Hand your list of references to the hiring manager during your job interview.

Send a copy of your resume to each person who has agreed to serve as a reference for you

Don't let them struggle to remember what you did on the job.

Send a copy of your resume plus a list of the projects or assignments you worked on together. Be sure to include your duties, responsibilities, accomplishments and any other information that might help them write a good recommendation for you.

Be sure to thank them for helping you. Oh, and do let them know when you receive a job offer.

QUESTIONS A HIRING MANAGER MIGHT ASK YOUR REFERENCES

- Were you Heidi Hopeful's immediate supervisor?
- What was Heidi's job title?
- What were her dates of employment?
- What were her duties and responsibilities?
- What were her most significant accomplishments?
- Did Heidi receive any promotions or awards?
- What was Heidi's attitude toward work?
- What was her level of energy at work?
- Did she get along with her coworkers and supervisors?
- How often was she late or absent?
- What were her job strengths?
- In which skills does Heidi need improvement?
- Why did Heidi leave the job?
- If possible, would you rehire her?
- Is there anything I didn't ask you, that I should have asked?

How to fill out a job application

On the next few pages, you'll find questions commonly asked on most job applications. Use these pages to create a "copy sheet" with accurate dates, names, addresses, and numbers. Later, when you fill out a real job application you won't struggle to remember the facts. You can simply copy the information from these pages.

If you haven't completed the company's standard job application yet, you'll be asked to complete one before your job interview begins.

The application is part of the paperwork. It's a record that shows you applied for a job. It's also a legal document— you are asked to sign a statement giving the employer permission to check the facts in your application.

The way you complete the application makes a statement about the kind of worker you are.

A complete, accurate, and neat application says that you take pride in your work.

Missing information and information entered in the wrong spaces, says that you didn't follow the instructions.

Misspelled names, partial addresses, wrong telephone numbers, and missing dates, say that you came unprepared.

Exaggerations make a statement about your truthfulness. When sitting across from the hiring manager, you don't want to be put in the awkward spot of having to admit that you embellished some of your answers.

Read the application carefully before you start. If you don't understand a question, ask for help. If a question does not apply to you, write "Not Applicable," or "N.A." in the space.

Sixty-eight percent of employers say that the best way to apply for an open position is through the employment page of their company's web site.

—The Society for Human Resource Management

A PRACTICE APPLICATION FOR EMPLOYMENT

PART 1. APPLICANT INFORMATION

Last name	First name	Middle initial

Address City State Zip

Telephone	Email or text address

Social Security Number

		Yes	No
Are you 18 years of age or older?		☐ Yes	☐ No
Are you a citizen of the United States?		☐ Yes	☐ No
Are you legally eligible for employment in the United States?		☐ Yes	☐ No

Have you served in the Armed Forces of the United States? ☐ Yes ☐ No

If "Yes" give dates	Branch of service	Highest rank

Duties

Are you now a member of the National Guard or the Reserves? ☐ Yes ☐ No

If "Yes" give dates	Branch of service	Rank

Duties

PART 2. EMPLOYMENT DESIRED

What position are you seeking?	Wage or salary expected

Note: Do not give a wage or salary. You might look unreasonable if it's too large, or look desperate if it's too low. Instead, write "Standard wage."

Are you seeking: ☐ Full-time work ☐ Part-time work ☐ Seasonal work

When can you begin work?

Which days can you work?	Monday	Tuesday	Wednesday	Thursday	Friday	Saturday	Sunday
Which hours can you work?							

Are you available for overtime? ☐ Yes ☐ No

If hired, will you have reliable transportation to and from work? ☐ Yes ☐ No

How were you referred to us?
- ☐ Friend or relative
- ☐ Our website
- ☐ State job center
- ☐ School career center
- ☐ Online job site. Name:

- ☐ "Now hiring" sign
- ☐ Newspaper advertisement
- ☐ Radio or TV advertisement
- ☐ Job fair
- ☐ Employment agency
- ☐ Other

Have you been employed with us in the past? ☐ Yes ☐ No

If "Yes," please give the following

Your job title	Supervisor's name
Department	Work address
Dates of employment	Reason for leaving

INFORMATION YOU'LL NEED TO COMPLETE A JOB APPLICATION

Your Information
- Your legal name
- Address
- Telephone
- Email
- Social Security Number
- Work permits
- Work licenses

Employee Friend
- Friend's name
- Job title
- Department
- Address
- Telephone

Each School
- School's name
- Address
- Telephone
- Your date of completion or attendance
- Degree, award, or major

Former Employers
- Company's name
- Address
- Telephone
- Your job title
- Begin/End dates
- Duties
- Supervisor's name

Three References
- Names
- Job titles
- Addresses
- Phone numbers
- Best times to call

Do you have a friend or relative employed by us? ☐ Yes ☐ No

Note: Having an inside friend recommend you is one of the best ways to get a job. But, always ask permission before you offer someone's name. Those who are asked, almost always give better recommendations than those who are not asked.

If "Yes," please provide the following information about your friend:

Person's name	Job title
Department	Work address
Phone	

PART 3. EDUCATION

High school attended

School's name	
AddressCityState Zip	
Years completed	Did you receive a diploma/GED? ☐ Yes ☐ No
Program or specialty	Grade Point Average (GPA):
Sports/Clubs/Groups	

College, university, or other post-secondary school attended

School's name	
AddressCityState Zip	
Years completed	Degree or certification awarded
Program or specialty	Grade Point Average (GPA)
Sports/Clubs/Groups	

PART 4. EMPLOYMENT

Note: If you have no formal work experience, don't panic. Instead, list the informal jobs you've had—volunteer, charitable, self-employment, freelance or homemaker. You can even list casual jobs like coaching, tutoring, baby-sitting, or mowing lawns

Current or last employer

Company name	
AddressCityState Zip	
Your job title	Your hourly wage or salary
Begin date	End date

Note: When listing your duties, include numbers from your resume on page 12 to turn your duties into accomplishments

Your duties

Supervisor's name	May we contact him or her? ☐ Yes ☐ No
Supervisor's telephone number	
Your reason for leaving	

Previous employer

Company name	
AddressCityState Zip	
Your job title	Your hourly wage or salary
Begin date	End date
Your duties	

Supervisor's name	May we contact him or her? ☐ Yes ☐ No
Supervisor's telephone number	
Your reason for leaving	

Previous employer

Company name ·
_____

AddressCityState Zip
_____

Your job title	Your hourly wage or salary

Begin date	End date

Your duties
_____
_____

Supervisor's name	May we contact him or her? ☐ Yes ☐ No

Supervisor's telephone number
_____

Your reason for leaving
_____

PART 5. REFERENCES

Note: A reference is someone who can testify to your character and abilities. Managers, supervisors, coworkers, customers, teachers, coaches, clergy, public officials, business leaders, and others not related to you, are acceptable references. Again, before you offer anyone's name as a reference, make sure you have that person's permission.

Personal reference #1

Person's name	Telephone

AddressCityState Zip
_____

How do you know this person?	Best time to call?

Personal reference #2

Person's name	Telephone

AddressCityState Zip
_____

How do you know this person?	Best time to call?

Personal reference #3

Person's name	Telephone

AddressCityState Zip
_____

How do you know this person?	Best time to call?

PART 6. ADDITIONAL INFORMATION

Please list any special skills, languages, qualifications, accomplishments, certifications, or licenses you have that were not previously mentioned
_____

Please give any additional information you feel may be helpful when considering your application
_____

PART 7. PLEASE READ CAREFULLY BEFORE SIGNING

I understand that this application for employment will be given every consideration, but its receipt does not constitute a contract of employment, nor does it imply that I will be hired.

I certify that all answers given on this employment application are true and complete. I also understand and agree that any false information may be grounds for termination of my employment at any point in the future if I am hired.

I understand that all information on this job application is subject to verification. I authorize and give my consent for Ajax Company to contact my references, educational institutions, previous employers, and to conduct all other necessary background checks.

I hereby acknowledge that I have read and understand this agreement.

Signature	Printed name	Date

BACKGROUND CHECKS

Most employers will try to verify the information given in your job application, resume, and job interview. Unless your state has legal restrictions, employers may also obtain the following information:

- Address history
- Character references
- Court records
- Credit records
- Driving records
- Drug tests
- Education records
- Employment history
- Licensing records
- Military records
- Neighbor interviews
- Past employers
- Personal references
- Sex offender lists
- Social Security Number
- Work permits
- Worker compensation claims

What to wear to a job interview and why it matters

Think about this—when you meet someone new, you size him or her up. In about a minute, you can decide whether or not you like the person. Well, hiring managers are good at sizing people up too. They see lots of job applicants and they can tell in a flash who will fit in and who will not. In a job interview, the goal is to show that you fit in—and the first thing a hiring manager will notice is how you look. Here's how to make a good, first impression:

Start with a good night's sleep

Employers expect to meet someone who is enthusiastic, energetic, and excited to be there.

Shower

It will help you look sharp, alert, and healthy.

Shampoo your hair

One of the first things the manager will look at is your hair. It makes a huge statement about your overall hygiene and cleanliness.

Brush your teeth

Get the manager to remember your ideas, your skills, your personality—not what you had for breakfast. Brush, floss, and use a mouthwash.

Use deodorant and an antiperspirant

The manager will think that you're as cool as a cucumber. Rub a little on your hands and you'll have a smooth dry handshake too.

Use eye drops

Get the red out and let your eyes twinkle.

Trim your nails

Guys, long fingernails are a turn off. Most hiring managers will notice when they reach to shake your hand. Ladies, hiring managers won't be impressed if long nails prevent you from doing the work.

Hair styles

Choose a simple style that makes you look good. Get the manager to focus on your face, your expressions, your eyes—not your hair style.

Right or wrong, people do make assumptions based on the way we dress. In 3 to 5 seconds, they make judgements about our confidence, character, income and sociability.

—Psychology Today

Avoid strong perfumes or colognes

Fragrances can linger and some people may find them annoying.

Makeup

In business, less is more. The idea is to look professional so you'll be taken seriously.

Shave

Guys, a two-day stubble looks great on the weekend, but not in a job interview. Showing up with stubble means you didn't shave.

Body piercings

One or two piercings are fine. A half dozen or more becomes a distraction. Tongue jewelry can also be a distraction.

Avoid trendy fashions

It's been said that fashion gets attention—but it doesn't convey power. Classic clothing conveys power. Conduct your job interview from a point of strength, not novelty.

Dress in the clothes that you would wear on the job

Executives should wear business suits. Office people should wear dress clothes. Workers should wear work clothes. If you're not sure what to wear to your interview, call the company and ask someone in their human resources office. They'll be glad to tell you.

You can't go wrong with the classic white-collar outfits

For men—navy-blue blazer, gray slacks, white shirt, striped tie, black lace-up shoes, black socks, and a black dress belt. For women—a charcoal gray or navy skirt or pantsuit, white blouse, scarf or necklace, with black pumps, black hose, black belt, and a simple black bag.

Check your clothes

Make sure they fit properly and feel comfortable. Check for holes, tears, splits, stains, missing buttons, runs, frayed hems, worn cuffs, puckers, pulls, or wrinkles.

Wear clean, freshly pressed clothes

Send your jacket, skirt, and pants off to be dry-cleaned and pressed. Have your shirt or blouse laundered, starched, and pressed. Looking sharp tells the manager that you take pride in your appearance and your work.

Avoid excessive jewelry

For men, a wristwatch and a ring are plenty. For women, a watch, a ring, a necklace, and a pair of earrings are ideal.

Avoid bright colors, loud fashions, and patterns that clash

It's another sign that you need lots of attention.

Empty your pockets

No bulges to ruin your profile and no jingling change to fall out of your pocket when you sit down for your interview.

Smile—smile big

You're beautiful. Take a picture!

Enthusiasm, the key to a great interview

Hiring managers agree—enthusiasm separates the winners from the losers. It can be more important than experience. "Give me someone who's enthusiastic and motivated," explained one manager, "someone who's alert and alive... someone who's interested in what we do here... someone who's excited about coming to work for me... someone who wants to help me as much as I want to help them."

You don't need to become one of the loud, back-slapping types

Just be yourself.

Plan to arrive ten-minutes early for your interview

It shows that you are excited to be there. Hiring managers are clock-watchers. They'll notice.

Be extra courteous

Say hello, smile, and be friendly to everyone you meet. You can bet that the manager will ask what they thought of you, after you've left the building.

Offer a professional greeting

When you meet the manager, stand up straight, look her in the eye, smile, extend a firm handshake, and say, "Ms. Joboffer, thank you so much for taking the time to interview me for your cat-herding position."

About that handshake

Engage the full hand, palm to palm. Grip firmly to show that you mean it, but don't crush. Look the other person in the eye. Smile. Pump two or three times. Release.

Don't undersell yourself and don't oversell yourself. Sales people who are middle-verts outsell introverts by 29 percent and outsell extraverts by 24 percent.

—Adam Grant, University of Pennsylvania

Show respect for the manager's position

Address the manager as Mr. or Ms., unless they ask you to call them by their first name. Once you're in the manager's office, don't sit down until you're invited to sit. Be sure to look at the manager whenever she speaks.

Show some curiosity

Ask for a short tour of the workplace before the interview begins. Look around. Ask questions about the cool things you see. Talk shop—ask what the manager thinks of the latest software, the newest gadget, or the hot new trend in your industry.

Have a sense of humor

We are drawn to happy, optimistic, humorous people. When appropriate, offer a clever quip, a one-liner, or an interesting tale. Keep it short, positive and upbeat. Don't forget to chuckle at the manager's attempts at humor.

Think, "can do"

If a manager says you don't have a certain skill or enough experience, don't just shrug your shoulders. Most managers want to see whether you'll fight for what you want or whether you'll just give up.

So, tell the hiring manager that you're a quick learner, a hard worker, and that you always deliver more than what's expected. Let her know that you will become one of the best employees she will ever hire.

Let your body language do some talking

Sit up straight. Sit near the edge of the chair with both feet on the floor. Visualize your ideas and use your hands to illustrate what you mean. Look the manager in the eye. Use facial expressions to emphasize important points.

Show a little empathy

Empathy means that you understand how the other person feels. When the manager talks about an important issue, look at her eyes to show that you are listening, use facial expressions to show that you understand, and ask for details to show that you care.

Have a reason for wanting to work there

Visit the company's website and Google the company name for news. Find out who they are, what they do, and why you want to work there.

Participate in the conversation

The interview should be a 50/50 conversation. Don't be a motor-mouth who never stops talking. And don't be a zombie who hardly says a word. Listen. Ask questions. Give generous answers.

Become a storyteller

You probably have a great reason for choosing your line of work. When the manager asks, "What made you decide to become a puppeteer?"— tell your story. Include lots of detail and use body language to bring your story to life.

TRY A LITTLE MIRRORING

Mirroring is a body-language dance where you copy the hiring manager's actions. It creates a bond. It says, "We're in sync."

Mirroring is not new. Everybody does it. If you smile at someone, they'll usually smile back. Like the smile, most mirroring is unintentional. But, if you are aware of mirroring, you can boost its effectiveness.

Here are some simple mirroring tips:

- When the hiring manager smiles or frowns, you should smile or frown too.
- If the manager uses hand gestures to add emphasis, you should use hand gestures when you want to add emphasis.
- If the manager sits up straight or leans toward you, you should sit straight or lean too.
- If the manager speaks quickly or slowly, you should match her pace when speaking.
- If the manager uses special job-related words or technical terms, you should use them too.

Navigate your way through a job interview

Managers are expert interviewers and they know that you're going to be nervous. To help you relax and feel comfortable, they'll conduct the interview as if it were a casual, friendly conversation. Now, each manager has her own style and personality. There is no set format to a job interview. But there is a beginning, a middle, and an end. So, let's walk through the interview from beginning to end and see how it unfolds.

• Your arrival

Come prepared for each interview. Don't wing it. Visit the company's website. Know who they are, what they do, and have a good reason why you want to work there.

When you first arrive, check in with the receptionist. Smile and introduce yourself. You might say, "Hi, my name is Luke Atmenow. I have a 4:14 appointment with Ms. Ida Hireyou in the Maple Syrup Department. When you have a moment could you please let her know that I'm here? Thank you."

If you're wearing a winter coat or a raincoat, ask where you can hang your coat. Don't bring it into the interview with you. You'll look awkward carrying it. Plus, carrying a coat gives the impression that this is a quick meeting and you'll be in and out in just a few minutes. Besides, what will you do with it once you're in the hiring manager's office? It's best if you hang your coat in the waiting room.

After checking your coat, visit the rest room. Check your hair, teeth, clothes and turn off your phone. Some hiring managers say they would not hire someone who took a cell call during a job interview.

Oh, while you're in the rest room, try this. Lock yourself into a stall. Then, strike the Superman pose. You know, feet apart, standing tall, hands on your hips, gazing upward. Hold that pose for two full minutes using a watch. You could walk into the interview feeling like you could change the world.

Seriously. A Harvard psychologist, Dr. Amy

The average job interview lasts about 55 minutes. Interviews for management-level positions last about 86 minutes.

—Robert Half Recruitment

Cutty, found that power posing reduced stress and increased confidence by about 20 percent.

Okay. Looking good? Feeling good? Phone turned off? Take a seat in the waiting area. Sit up straight. Try not to fidget. Run through the interview in your mind. Visualize the important points you'd like to make—like an athlete might visualize an upcoming event.

• The greeting

The hiring manager will usually come into the waiting area to meet you. Sometimes an assistant will greet you and escort you to hiring manager's office.

Either way, when someone mentions your name, stand up. Smile and say, "Hi, I'm Luke Atmenow." The hiring manager will smile, walk toward you and introduce herself.

Offer your handshake and say, "It's so nice to meet you, Ms. Hireyou. Thank you for inviting me to this interview." Saying her name will help you remember it.

As you are escorted to the hiring manager's office, make small talk to show that you are friendly and sociable. But, find something other than the weather or the traffic to chat about. Hiring managers hear the same weather/traffic chatter from hundreds of different job hunters.

Instead, explain why you are so thrilled to be interviewing with this company—and mean it. Make a good first impression and you'll set the tone for a good interview.

Another tip: If the hiring manager is escorting you to her office, ask for short tour to see the inner workings before the interview starts. Most people won't ask for a tour. If you do, the hiring manager will be impressed that you're interested—and that you asked. Plus,

a short tour will give you a chance to establish a rapport with the hiring manager and gain an insight into her personality, before the Q&A starts.

• The start

Once you're both seated in the hiring manager's office, the manager will lean forward, smile and say, "Okay, tell me a little about yourself."

That's one of the most common opening questions. And, it's the perfect time to deliver your fifteen-second sales pitch from page 23. Your pitch is quick, to the point, and it will show the hiring manager, right off, that you have the stuff she's looking for.

When you've finished delivering your pitch, offer the hiring manager your typed list of references. In return, ask for her business card. Asking for her business card is important—her business card will have all the information you'll need to follow-up after the interview is over.

Next, ask the hiring manager this— "Why did you invite me here today? What was it about my resume that led you to bring me in?"

Dr. Robert Cialdini, of Arizona State University, is an expert on influence. He states that the hiring manager will then glance at her notes and say, "Because of x and because of y."

This is important—the hiring manager is telling you what they found encouraging about your background and why he or she is interested in you.

The hiring manager will likely explain what interested them by saying, "I see here, on your resume, that you were the over-and-under guy at Round & Round. Can you tell me about your duties there?"

BECOME A STORY TELLER

Instead of explaining how or why you did something, try telling it as a story. Stories bring events to life.

A good story has three main parts, the beginning, middle, and end.

Another way to look at a good story is problem, struggle, outcome.

The problem, struggle, and outcome raise the energy of the story and make it more interesting.

Here's a little format you can use to craft your story.

· *Problem.* "I worked with some very difficult customers. For example…"

· *Struggle.* "I tried…, I tried…, I also tried…"

· *Outcome.* "Then one day…"

Keep your stories short and simple, about a minute or two each. Use your hands, facial expressions, and voice to bring them to life. Add a little humor whenever you can.

Stories can help you stand out. Long after you've left the interview, the hiring manager may not remember your name, but she'll remember your interesting story. "Hmmm," she'll think, "Maybe I should call that person who worked with all those difficult customers."

Keep in mind that your resume simply lists your accomplishments. It does not explain the back-stories on those accomplishments. This is your chance to tell those stories.

So, use your fingers and quickly count off your five main duties. 1-2-3-4-5. Then, have a short, interesting back-story prepared for each of those accomplishments. Toot your horn. The stage is yours.

• The Q&A

By now you are probably warmed up and feeling a bit more confident. So, the hiring manager will start to ask some probing questions. She'll dig a little deeper into your work projects to measure your skills, personality, and judgment.

There are two types of questions the hiring manager will ask, common and behavioral. Common questions require a simple answer, "Can you work weekends?" Behavioral questions require some thought, "What would you do if one manager told you to do something and another manager told you not to do it?"

Hiring managers ask behavioral questions, not to trick or embarrass you, but to see how you think, solve problems, and sort things out. There's usually no right or wrong answer.

There are fifty questions on pages 44 and 45 —both common and behavioral. There are also suggestions on how to answer them.

Spend some time on those questions. Come up with a good answer for each one. Write them down on flash cards and quiz yourself. You could also rehearse with a friend to verbalize your answers and get the kinks out before you go on the interview.

Now, if your conversation with the hiring manager slides into an awkward silent spot, weave in some questions of your own to create the ebb and flow of a two-way conversation. You might ask—

- "What are the department's goals for the year?"
- "What are the major challenges the new hire will face in this job?"
- "If hired, how long should it take for me to get my feet on the ground and become productive?"
- "Who are the key people I'd be working with and what do they do?"
- "Which employee do you rely upon most? What does she do and what makes her so reliable?"
- "How would I get feedback on my performance?"
- "How soon do you plan to fill this job?"

One thing, though, don't ask questions about wages, benefits, or vacations. To paraphrase President Kennedy, "Ask not what the company can do for you, show what you can do for the company." Besides, wages and benefits are usually discussed when the job offer is made.

• The close

Eventually, the conversation will start to slow down and the hiring manager will ask if you have any final questions. This is a sign that the interview is about to end.

Most of your questions will already be answered. But, you do want one or two solid, final questions up your sleeve. A good final question leaves a good final impression. Here are two:

- You could offer the manager a thirty-day trial period to prove yourself. It's a gutsy move that very few job hunters will offer. But it tells the hiring manager that you really want this job—and she'll remember that.

- You could also ask, "How much autonomy or self-direction would I have on the job?" This shows that you're responsible, a self-starter, the type of person who gets things done—a rare breed, a good catch.

When the hiring manager stands up, the interview is over. You should also stand. Then, look the hiring manager in the eye, smile, offer your handshake, and thank her for taking the time to meet with you.

Now, most job hunters never say whether they want the job or not, so make sure you do. You could simply say, "I'm pleased with what I've learned today. I want this position. Where do we go from here?"

The manager will probably say, "I'm still interviewing other candidates, I'll let you know."

Ask if you could follow up in a week, by phone, to see if she's made a decision

As she walks you to the door, say thanks again and add, "I hope you'll call *me*."

And that's it.

SO, HOW'D YOU DO IN THERE?

Grade your interview with this easy scoring system:
1 = Needs much more work
2 = Just OK— room for improvement
3 = Total win

Did you do your homework and know who the employer is, what they do, and why you want to work there?
1　**2**　**3**

Did you know which skills were required for the job and show the manager that you are a good fit for that job?
1　**2**　**3**

Did you offer examples to show that you are a hard worker and that you deliver more than the minimum?
1　**2**　**3**

Did you answer tough questions without stumbling or getting flustered?
1　**2**　**3**

Did you ask questions to learn more about the company and the job?
1　**2**　**3**

Did you look the manager in the eye and speak clearly?
1　**2**　**3**

Did you wear the proper clothes and look your best?
1　**2**　**3**

Did you show enthusiasm, a sense of humor, and a positive attitude?
1　**2**　**3**

Were you polite and respectful throughout the interview?
1　**2**　**3**

Did you ask for the job?
1　**2**　**3**

Add up your score. A perfect score is 30. Work on those areas where you need improvement. Think of every interview as practice for the next one.

50 questions to expect during your job interview

1. "Can you tell me a little about yourself?"
Give your 15-second sales pitch from page 23. After you've given your sales pitch, hand the hiring manager a fresh copy of your resume plus your typed list of references. Next, this is important—ask for the hiring manager's business card. That business card will have all of the manager's contact information, including her email address and direct phone number. You'll need this information so you can stay in touch with the hiring manager after the interview is over.

2. "Tell me what you know about my company."
Before you go on the interview, be sure to visit the company's website. Get an overview of the company's key products and services. Google the company name for news. Find out who they are, what they do, and why you want to work for them.

3. "Why did you decide to become a snake charmer?"
Tell your story. Include lots of detail and use body language to bring your story to life. Add a touch of humor when appropriate.

4. "What skills or requirements do you think are needed for this job?"
Refer back to page 11. Use your fingers and count off the requirements: 1... 2... 3... 4... 5...

5. "What motivates you to do a good job?"
Money is not a good answer. Instead, try this: "Having responsibilities and getting a pat on the back when the job is done right."

6. "Why is customer service so important in business today?"
"Customers who receive helpful service from friendly employees are more apt to come back again and again. They are also more apt to tell their friends about us. Good service means more business."

7. "Why should I hire you instead of someone more qualified?"
Toot your horn. Tell the manager that you have more than good skills to offer— you're a team player, you're not afraid of hard work, you're a quick learner, you're reliable, you give more than just the minimum effort, and— you want to work for this company because...

8. "Did you ever have a disagreement with your boss?"
Answer "yes" and you're a troublemaker, answer "no" and you're a wimp. Find the middle ground: "Sure we disagreed. But we worked well together. For example... "

9. "Tell me about the toughest boss you ever worked for."
Never badmouth a former boss. it says you're a troublemaker. Instead, turn

20. "What's your favorite book or movie? Why?"
Stay away from controversial issues.

21. "As a youngster, what did you do to earn your own spending money?"
Baby-sitting, lemonade stand, newspaper route, shoveling snow, mowing lawns, and other jobs show early signs of ambition and a respect for work.

22. "What do you do to relax after work?"
Don't brag about auto racing, bungee jumping, chain-saw juggling, or any other dangerous activity. They suggest a likelihood of injury and an absence from work. Instead, mention something wholesome like athletics, a hobby, a project, traveling, or entertaining friends.

23. "Are you at your best when working alone or in a group?"
"Both. I enjoy working as part of a team and I can work independently to get my share of the work done. For example.. "

24. "Would you rather be in charge of a project or work as part of the team?"
"Either. I'm not afraid to take responsibility and I'm not afraid to roll up my sleeves and pitch in."

25. "Have you ever been fired from a job?"
Everybody gets fired from a job at least once in their lifetime. And don't be afraid to tell the truth if it was your fault. Fessing up says that you are a responsible, mature adult. Explain what happened. Explain what you learned. Explain what you would do differently if the same situation happened again.

26. "Tell me about your strengths."
From page 11, you know the five or six requirements needed for the job you want. Choose your strongest job requirements and offer examples to show how you excelled.

27. "What are your weaknesses?"
Choose one or two weaknesses that are not part of the job requirements. Be sure to include an action point to show what you did about each weakness. For instance, "I'm terrified of public speaking. I get so nervous I start to shake. So, I took a stand-up comedy class to help get over the jitters—and entertain my friends."

28. "Tell me about your favorite accomplishment."
A personal touch works well here. You could also offer something both personal and benevolent. "I'm no athlete, but I did run a 5 kilometer road race in under 45 minutes—and I raised over $1,000 in pledges for a favorite charity. I'm proud of that."

36. "If you were told to report to a supervisor who was a woman, a minority, or someone with a physical disability, what problems would this create for you?"
"I don't see any problems. I genuinely like people. I'm easy to coach and I'm easy to work with. For example..."

37. "Tell me, what would you do if one supervisor told you to do something, and another supervisor told you not to do it?"
The manager wants to see how you would handle a dilemma. Try this: Think about what would happen if you did act. and what would happen if you did not act. Write down the pros and cons of each. Make a decision.

38. "Tell me about a time when you broke the rules."
Sometimes it's necessary to break the rules. Just make sure your reasoning and judgement are sound.

39. "Can you tell me about a time when a supervisor was not pleased with your work?"
The manager wants to know how you react to criticism. Here are a few tips to keep in mind when preparing your answer: Top employees see criticism as a learning experience, not a reprimand. They listen without arguing or becoming defensive. They learn what needs to be done differently. They agree to the changes and implement them. They follow up by asking the supervisor for a critique of their new work. They also regain their enthusiasm and confidence quickly.

40. "Tell me about a time when you were swamped with work and how you handled it."
The manager wants to know how you prioritize your time. Experts suggest you start by making a list of all the tasks you need to do today. Next, arrange those tasks from most important to least important. Then, select the task which is most urgent. Start there.

41. "Please tell me about a time when you showed initiative at work."
Initiative is not about working harder. Initiative is about doing more than what your job requires. For example: Taking on a new responsibility without being asked, taking a class or reading a book to learn a new skill, or noticing a problem on the horizon and taking action to correct it.

42. "Describe a difficult decision you had to make."
The manager wants to know about your decision-making skills. Here's a basic decision-making formula: Define the problem. learn what others did in similar situations. list the pros and cons for each option, then choose the best option.

43. "Tell me about a time when you failed."
Everybody fails. What's important is the lesson learned from the failure. Keep these tips in mind when planning your answer. Describe the event.

a negative into a positive. "That would be Mr. Gray. He was a demanding, detail-driven perfectionist. But, I learned more from him than anyone I've ever worked with. For example…"

10. "What salary or wage are you looking for?"
Get the manager to throw out the first figure. Ask, "What salary or wage do you usually offer someone with my skills and abilities?"

11. "Tell me about your current (or last) job."
Give the company's name and what they do. Give your job title. List your duties and responsibilities. Explain your accomplishments.

12. "Why are you leaving that job?"
Job stagnation, demotions due to downsizing, or simply having made a poor choice are all good reasons.

13. "What will your manager say when you give notice that you're leaving?"
Explain why you'll be missed. Don't give the impression that they'll be glad to be rid of you.

14. "Did you enjoy school?"
The manager wants to know if you enjoy learning and whether you might benefit from a training program.

15. "In school, which course did you find most difficult?"
The manager wants to know if you have perseverance: "My first term in history, I got a D. My study skills were all wrong, so I joined a study group. By second term I pulled it up to a B and kept it there."

16. Did you participate in any school activities?"
School activities show that you're sociable. They show that you enjoy being part of a group and that you can work with other people. This is important in the work place.

17. "Do you plan to continue your education?"
Adding to your education says that you want to grow and prosper, professionally as well as personally.

18. "What do you hope to get out of this job?"
Try this—"A reasonable paycheck, responsibility for doing something that matters, a say in how my work is done, recognition by my coworkers for being good at what I do, and a pat on the back from the boss for doing a good job."

19. "Last year, how many days of work (or school) did you miss? How many days were you late?"
This will tell the manager whether you're going to show up for work on time every day. If you've missed more than a few days, have some good explanations ready.

29. "Who did you ask to serve as personal references and why did you choose them?"
"I chose a good mix—a former boss who can tell you about my skills and job performance—a coworker who can tell you about the hard work, and extra effort we put in as a team—and a former coach who can tell you that I'm not only a good team player, I can work independently and I always complete my share of the work."

30. "What are the three things you look for when considering a new job?"
The things that make people happiest at work are not always about money and benefits. Experts say that the following things are often more important: being appreciated, earning respect, being trusted, taking on new challenges, having a good boss, working with people you enjoy, and making a difference.

31. "How are you unique?"
Try this: "I'm a quick learner, a hard worker. I'm easy to coach, and I always deliver more than what's expected. I could be one of the best employees you'll ever hire."

A The following include some behavioral questions. Behavioral questions help the manager see how you might act or behave in certain situations.

32. "Tell me how you keep a positive attitude when the job gets stressful?"
Here's how positive people stay positive: They know that attitude is a choice. They choose to plan ahead and schedule the time needed to get things done. They choose to be around other positive people. They choose to laugh and have a sense of humor. They choose to be friendly and helpful to everyone. They choose to offset negative thoughts by looking for the positive points.

33. "Please tell me about a time when you had to motivate a coworker."
Some of the best motivational tools include praise and encouragement, giving a helpful demonstration or example, explaining the rewards of the job, and brainstorming for better ways to do the job.

34. "Can you tell me about a goal you set for yourself?"
The manager wants to know if you set goals. People who set goals are more productive than those who do not set goals. The best goals are specific, measurable, and plausible. For example, "I want to pay off my $1,000 car loan in six months," is a better goal than, "I want to pay off my car loan quickly."

35. "Describe a problem you faced and how you solved that problem."
Think of something related to work, school, sports, or volunteering. Tell it as a story. The manager wants to see how you: 1) Define the problem, 2) Identify options and, 3) Decide on a solution.

describe the goal you hoped to achieved, describe the failed outcome, explain what went wrong, and explain the lesson learned from the failure.

44. "Describe a time when you had to work with a difficult person."
The manager wants to see how you interact with moody, lazy, or obnoxious people. Ideally, you are a peacemaker who tries to resolve conflicts. When provoked, you have a private talk with the person. You remain pleasant. You explain how the behavior makes you feel. And you try to reach an agreement with the culprit.

45. "Please tell me about a time when you were disappointed."
The manager isn't so much interested in what happened, but what you did about that disappointment. Try something like this. "When I didn't get the promotion—I was surprised and hurt. But, I swallowed my pride and congratulated the winner—she earned that promotion. The next day, I reviewed my work performance. I redoubled my efforts, and I haven't missed a promotion since."

46. "Tell me about a project you worked on."
The manager wants to know about your role in the project, specifically what you did. Begin by describing the project and the project's goal. Then, describe the team you worked with, specifically your duties, your responsibilities, your contribution, and any new skills you learned. Finally, tell whether the project met its goals.

47. "Tell me where you expect to be 5 years from now?"
Try this: "It's hard to know where anyone will be five years from now. But, I am looking for a company where I'll be appreciated, trusted, and able to make a difference. I want to work with people I enjoy, people who challenge me, and a good boss who's not afraid to tell us we did a good job. I think your company might be the one I'm looking for. That's why I'm here today."

48. "Are there any questions I didn't ask, that I should have asked?"
This is a great time to bring up any special skill, ability, or accomplishment that wasn't discussed.

49. "Okay, you've got one minute to convince me that you're the best person for this job. Begin."
Do it in only 30 seconds and you'll make a big impression. Start by delivering your 15-second sales pitch. Then, spend 15 seconds explaining why you want to work for this company. End by asking for the job.

50. "Do you have any questions for me?"
On page 42, you'll find a list of questions to ask the hiring manager. Add a few questions of your own to the list.

The Job Hunting Handbook, Copyright 2020 Harry Dahlstrom

The art of the follow-up

When you get home from your interview, send the manager a thank-you note. Two days later, send the manager an *idea* note. A week after your interview, pick up the phone and give the manager a call.

1. Send a thank-you note

Most job hunters do send thank-you notes. You should send them too.

Keep in mind that businesses are formal. Manners are important. Thank-you notes are expected. Managers look for these things.

Keep your thank-you note brief.

· Thank the manager for meeting with you and mention the date and job title you interviewed for.

· Say that you want the job.

· Give one or two solid reasons why the hiring manager should offer you the job.

· Offer the manager a thirty-day trial period to prove yourself.

· Say that you'd like to call in a week or so to see if she's made a decision.

Write your thank-you note and send it off within 24 hours of the interview while the manager stills remembers you.

2. Send an idea note

Now, here's something hardly any of your competitors will try—

During your interview, the manager asked if you had any questions for her. You said, "Yes, what are the major challenges the new hire will face in this job?"

Now, think about the manager's answer. If the problems are not confidential, discuss them with a friend or look for a solution online. Come up with a few suggestions. Then, send the

Sixty percent of hiring managers say it's important for a job hunter to send a thank-you note after a job interview.

—Society for Human Resource Management

manager a short note explaining your ideas.

Your suggestions don't have to be brilliant, just good. The point is, the manager will see that you're a problem solver and that you were the only one who made an extra effort to win the job offer.

Send your idea note a day or so after your thank-you note, but before you follow-up on the telephone.

3. Call the manager

A week after your interview, call the manager to see if she's made a decision. Yes, every-body hates making these calls. But, it shows that you're the kind of person who gets things done—even if the task is unpleasant.

Pick up the phone and make the call.
"Good morning, Ms. Hireyou. This is Emma Gogetter. I wanted to call and thank you for meeting with me last week about your lion tamer's position."

Ask if the manager has made a decision.
"I'm very interested in that position and I thought I'd follow-up to see if you've made a decision."

If you got the job—
"Really? Yikes—Thank you! (Hey Ma...!")

"When would you like me to start?"

"What time should I report?"

"Where should I report?"

"To whom should I report?"

"What do I need to bring with me on the first day?"

If the manager hasn't yet made a decision—
"Am I still a candidate for consideration?"

"I'd love to have this job. Would you consider giving me a trial period to prove myself?"

If she needs time to think it over, ask—"Would it be okay if I call back on Friday?"

When you do call back and the manager says, "We offered the job to someone else"—
Don't beg, don't lose your cool, and don't close any doors. You might say—

"Gee, I'm sorry to hear that."

"Ms. Hireyou, I'd like to thank you for your time and consideration. It was a pleasure to meet you and to learn about your company."

"If the person you chose for this job becomes unavailable, please call me. I'd be happy to come in for another interview."

IF YOU DIDN'T GET THE JOB— STAY IN TOUCH

Once or twice a month, send every hiring manager you've met a short note and another copy of your resume. Let them know that you are still available and that you are still interested in working for them.

Remember, jobs open up all the time. Some people decline job offers. Some change their minds and quit. Other people don't work out and management will let them go.

Sometimes jobs also open up in other departments as well. Most managers are eager to refer solid applicants to other hiring managers.

So, stay in touch with all your hiring managers. They are your inside connection—and a gentle persistence can re-open doors. The idea is to become the first person they think of when something new opens up.

The Short Course

People change jobs all the time. Some quit, some transfer to other departments, some are fired, some retire. Employers are always looking for good people to hire. Even during the worst recessions, it's amazing how quickly a hiring freeze will thaw when the right person starts chipping away the ice.

Show employers that you have the right stuff.

Read some help-wanted ads for your occupation to see which skills and requirements today's hiring managers want. Then, create a job application, resume, cover letter, and sales pitch that offer what most employers are looking for.

Make a list of all the people you know who have jobs in the same field or occupation that you want to work in.

When filling job openings, nine out of ten employers prefer to hire the friends of their trusted employees. Reach out to your friends who work in your field. Ask if they would give your resume to their hiring managers and put in a good word for you.

Contact five new employers every day.

Every employer is not hiring today. You have to knock on a lot of doors to find the ones who are. So, in addition to contacting friends who work in the industry where you would like to work, apply for jobs posted on employer websites, as well as those listed on job sites like Indeed, Careerbuilder, and Monster. Then, attend some job fairs, sign up with a temporary employment agency, and check the job listings at your school and state job centers.

If a hiring manager likes what she sees in your resume or job application, she'll give you a call.

During this phone call, she will ask a few questions about your background and availability. If the manager thinks you are a good fit for the job, she'll invite you to a face-to-face job interview.

Managers are expert interviewers and they know that you'll be nervous.

To help you relax and feel comfortable, they'll conduct the interview as if it were a casual, friendly, conversation. But, you need to be prepared. Dress appropriately. Be respectful. Have a sense of humor. Show some enthusiasm. Have a good answer for each of the 50 questions a hiring manager might ask. If you want the job, be sure to ask for it.

When you get home from your interview, send the hiring manager a thank-you note.

A few days later, follow-up with a short letter offering an idea, a clarification, or an insight into something discussed during your interview. A week after the interview, call the hiring manager to see if you got the job.

If you get the job—*Congratulations!*

If you didn't get the job, here's a tip.

Continue to contact five new employers every day. Plus, stay in touch with all the hiring managers you have met. Once or twice a month, send those managers a fresh copy of your resume, plus a short note to let them know that you are still interested in working with them.

Keep in mind that jobs open up all the time and a gentle persistence can pay off.

The idea is to become the first person they think of when something new becomes available.

Best wishes, Harry Dahlstrom